Carried Away

Carried Away
Copyright © 2025 Stacia Leigh
All rights reserved.

This is a work of fiction. Names, characters, places, and incidents are products of the author's imagination or are used fictitiously and are not to be construed as real. Any resemblance to actual events, locales, organizations, people or persons, living or dead, is entirely coincidental.

The excerpts from *Dealing with Blue* and *Burnout* (originally titled *Riding with the Hides of Hell*) and *Hanging Around for You*, the cover design, photography, stories, poetry, and art are by:

Stacia Leigh at www.espialdesign.com

No part of this book may be reproduced or distributed in any printed or electronic form without prior written permission by Stacia Leigh, except in the case of brief quotations embodied in reviews.

Help support independent authors and artists! Purchase only authorized editions and discourage piracy of copyrighted materials.

ISBN-13: 978-1-7321435-3-1

ALSO BY STACIA LEIGH

♥

Dealing with Blue

Burnout

Hanging Around for You

Sounds Complicated: Blackout Poetry and Art

Distance Between: Blackout Poetry and Art

♥

To a couple skilled artists
and a very special computer nerd.

Carried Away

Blackout Poetry and Art

by
Stacia Leigh

GOOSEBUMPS

The world wanted to see you.
Even the dirt was covered in goosebumps.

One-Word Prompt: Curve

Stacia Leigh

out of a graceful face-plant and jerked up to stand in front of him. She looked hot-and-bothered with a sharp finger pointed right at his chest and ready for damage.

But before she could jab him, he gently grabbed her wrist and guided her toward him.

"Man, you drive me crazy," he murmured. His body tingled at the world of Suzy surrounding him.

"What?" Suzy's eyes bugged, and she shoved him away. "I can't believe you. You need to leave...now."

"I like being in your space. Look, I'm covered in goosebumps." He held out his arm. What a trip.

Here he stood, completely affected by her, and she glared at him. She was tough, man. Even outright flirting with her hit the dirt, and teasing wasn't getting him anywhere, either. Cool it, man. Be yourself, but be normal. J.J. glanced around her bedroom, committing it to memory.

"I like your room," he said.

"Shh. Keep your voice down. My mom's out there. Ugh." Suzy covered her eyes and groaned. "You're trespassing."

He waved that away. "I wanted to see you...to talk...to say I'm sorry."

"So talk." She crossed her arms under her chest and cocked her hip out to one side.

"Alright..." J.J. shrugged, and before he could stop himself, he asked, "Where've you been anyway? (Sunday

Goosebumps by Stacia Leigh   9/20/18

THE FOURTH WALL

Officially, starting another observation of the wall.
It was an exercise in staring.

🚩 *One-Word Prompt: Stack*

Dealing with Blue

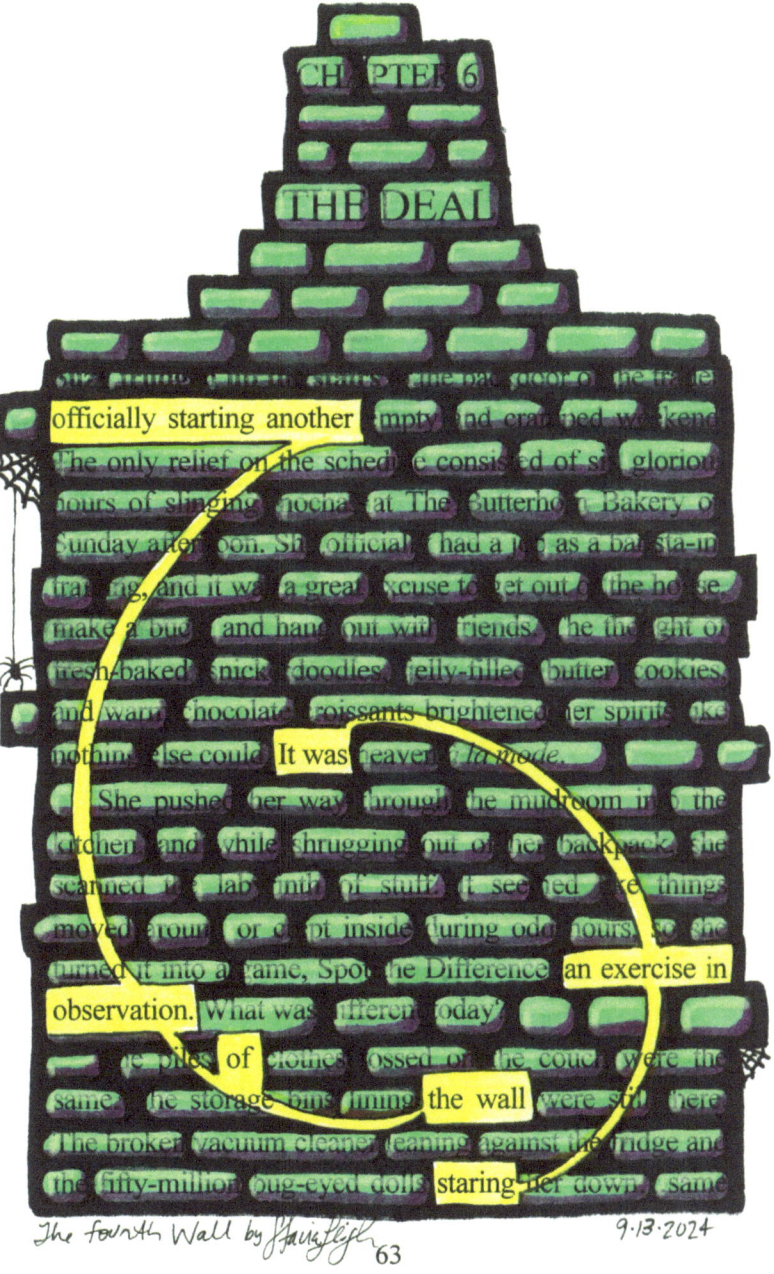

officially starting another ... It was heaven ... an exercise in observation. ... the wall ... staring

POTION PANTRY

Night, stubble, jaw, death.
Sigh, problems, snacks.
Worth the trouble, shadows, crawling.

One-Word Prompt: Shelf

Potion Pantry by Stacia Leigh 4/5/2020

YES, YES, YES

Everything's yes, yes, yes
until the games end.

⚑ *One-Word Prompt: Block*

TOP OF THE MORNING

The sun rose,
and his windpipe burned.

🏳 *One-Word Prompt: Wake*

Stacia Leigh

"No." Will ran and scooped it up. "Keep it!" He turned, holding it toward the window; it was empty. This time, she really was gone. "Miki?" Will said softly and let his arm drop. If she was still there...

Nothing.

There was only the whirring fan and the put-put-puttering of Pitty's lips as he started to snore softly.

"Stay safe, Miki."

How long would it take her to get down the mountain? Would she meet any of the Hides of Hell on her way? Did the guys even know they were trapped? What if she ran into the Silver Skulls? What would they do to her?

Will bit the skin on his chapped lips. He wouldn't be able to help her; he wouldn't know if she made it or not.

A big ball of pain the size of the sun rose out of his chest, and his windpipe burned with loss. No air. Tears leaked out of his eyes. Snot dripped from his nose. Shortly after came the sweat and the shakes. Everything hurt, inside and out.

He closed his lids, slid down the gray wall, and cried while trying to hold it all in.

After a long, catatonic state of nothingness, a buzzing sound brought him back into consciousness. *Buzz-buzz-buzz.* Silence. On again, off again. He slapped at his hip, expecting to feel a vibrating phone in a denim pocket but found neither. Instead, he was flat on his back in his Ghetto Gramps ready to make angels on the dirty floor. The sun sat low in the sky and reflected off the busted

Top of the Morning by Stacia Leigh 1/2/20

CAT MAN

Never once had wrecking his heart
made him want a cat.
Things change.

One-Word Prompt: Pet

Dealing with Blue

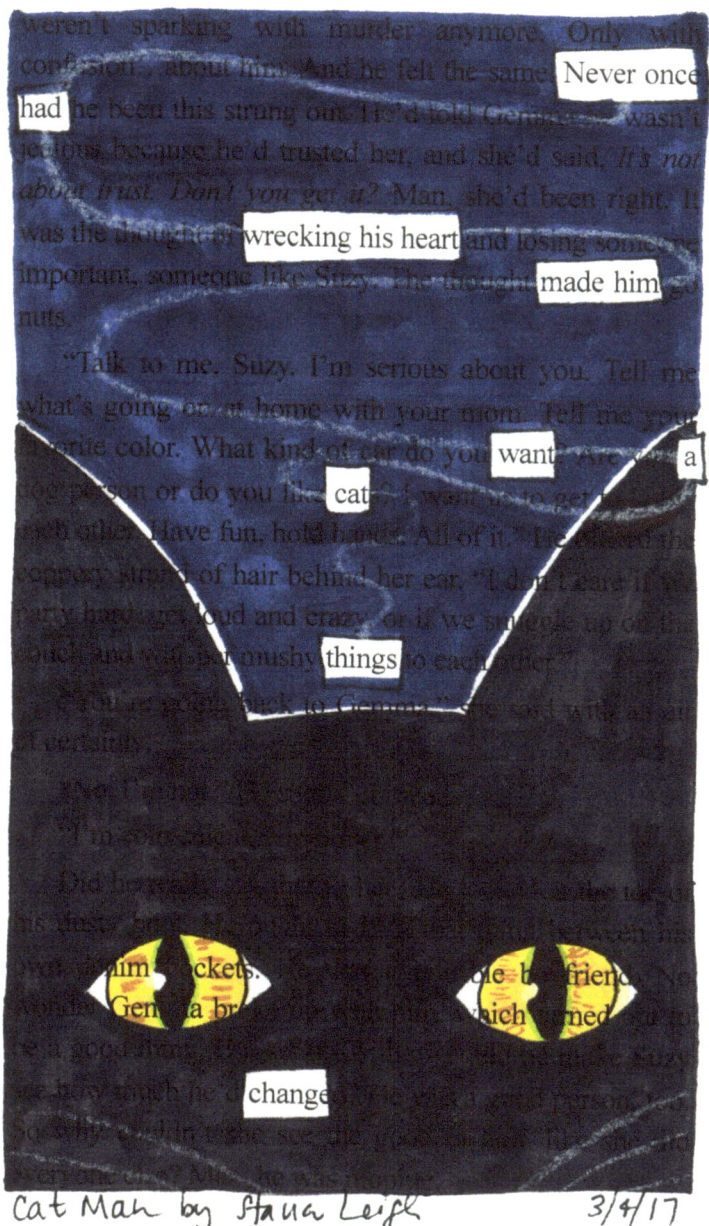

ZOOM

I'm talking about
the jokes of the past.

🚩 *One-Word Prompt: Connect*

Stacia Leigh

"I'm talking about when you ran out of your house this morning. You looked ready to burst. Is everything okay at home, you know, with your mom?"

Suzy dropped her head and studied her shoes. Ugh, shut up. She was not going to discuss her home life with Mr. Cool La la la. Maybe if she stared at her feet long enough, J.J. would give up and go away. In fact, look at that, a scuff on her left toe from where she'd fallen in the gravel. Proof that nothing stayed nice for long.

"C'mon, Blue, you're my girlfriend, remember? Let's walk to class together, and if you play nice..." He nudged her. "...I'll let you drive my truck."

Suzy looked up, and her heart fluttered at his long, dark lashes and warm gaze. It was the last class of the day, and for all the dread she packed with her through the halls, not one single person looked at her funny or made J.J.-saw-your-totas jokes. She heard no snickers or whisperings of Blue's hooters, headlamps, or blinkers, so maybe she would get through this unscathed. J.J. didn't seem like such a bad guy after all. Maybe she could trust him.

"Driving...is that our first date?"

"Yeah..." He grinned and pushed off the locker. "...and don't forget the rules, ten and two on the wheel and no pawing." Suzy's face burned as he glanced past her, searching for Gemma, no doubt, who must be close. Otherwise, he wouldn't be wasting his time. "But if you

Zoon by Stacia Leigh   5·24·20

130

UNDER THE WEATHER

Mount Saint Helens had a cramp.

One-Word Prompt: Place

Stacia Leigh

Mount Saint Helens.

cramp

Under the Weather by Stacia Leigh   2/25/18

A PICK ME UP

You should feel honored,
while hopefully, I won't remember a thing.

One-Word Prompt: Insult

"You should feel honored.

While

hopefully, I won't remember a thing.

a Pick Me Up by Staira Leigh   6/20/18

IN THE DARK

The dirt dad was down,
disgust in the dust.
"Grow! Grow!"

One-Word Prompt: Alliteration

Stacia Leigh

the dirt.

dad

down

disgust.

in the dust

grow,

In the Dark by Stacia Leigh   12·29·18

CARRIED AWAY, AGAIN

I like to sleep
and imagine a world carried away.

One-Word Prompt: Sky

Carried Away, Again by Stacia Feigh 9/20/18

SHEEPLE

Before you go,
enlighten me.

One-Word Prompt: Divide

Stacia Leigh

BOLD

The wish included a piping hot moment of truth.

⚐ One-Word Prompt: Drink

Stacia Leigh

CHAPTER 19

ENTER SANDMAN

J.J. stretched his denim legs along the back cushions of the overstuffed couch, his feet reaching Suzy's loose coppery curls. She didn't move. She lay beside him, her head at the opposite end, dead to the world. At least part of his wish had come true; he got to cuddle with Suzy in front of the TV. But they couldn't very well play nurse when his parents, Monty included, hovered nearby. And as it turned out, Suzy wasn't really all that sympathetic about his broken wing, because—she twitched against him, her eyelids closed, and her mouth open—she was off in dreamland.

Cute.

J.J. studied Suzy's pert nose covered with a mist of freckles. Didn't she care about missing his new favorite show? The tatted chef with barbells in his face pulled out a piping hot loaf of manna bread with his studded black oven mitt. Would the devil's biker-baker buddies devour or destroy the loaf? It was the moment of truth, yet Suzy snored softly with her bare feet in J.J.'s face. His hand rested warmly around her toes, and he smiled.

Bold by Stacia Leigh   11·08·18

262

IT'S TIME

It's about trust,
time to step through the fire.

One-Word Prompt: Step

"It's about trust. Time to step through the fire.

It's Time by Stacia Leigh   9.19.18

FOR A GOOD TIME CALL

Everyone knows his number.
It was written on a big truck.

One-Word Prompt: Lettering

BUZZED ON THE COFFEE

Buzzed on the coffee…
watching, busy, grinning.
Stop thinking!

One-Word Prompt: Tape

THE FALL

The moment to process life
with a sudden release...

🏳 *One-Word Prompt: Season*

Stacia Leigh

CHAPTER 18

UNRAVELING

Thirsty. Dirty. Hungry. Face-down in the muck. Completely exhausted. Miki's hands were free, buried under a blanket of dead leaves, and even though she could push off the ground anytime she pleased, she didn't. A single moment to process her life was required. Her muscles ached. They were limp. Shaky. Yet, overall, she was supremely relieved to be in the position she was in.

"Have I told you lately that I love you?" she whispered hoarsely to the weight on her back.

"I told you to shut up," Owen growled, still sitting on her rump, pinning her down. "Listen. Hear that?" he asked with a strained voice. She could hear jack squat, only the blood pumping in her ears.

"All clear," someone whispered loudly from another hiding spot. It had to be Flossy. Was Trip here, too?

The sudden release of anxiety and fear gushed through her system, and tears flooded her eyes. They spilled over and flowed warmly across her skin, plip-plipping off the end of her nose. She was surrounded by her men, her family. She'd found help.

The Fall by Stacia Leigh   5·3·20

A BEAUTIFUL LAUGH

The joker stood with tears.
A beautiful laugh said,
We're going to get through it.

🏳 *One-Word Prompt: Humor*

Stacia Leigh

There was skin and cleavage and no straps and joked over stood with tears beautiful laughed Suzy said we're going to get through it.

A Beautiful Laugh by Stacia Leigh   July 8, 2017

PLAY GAMES

Play games with a pig
and encourage jeers.

Oink.

⚑ *One-Word Prompt: Game*

Stacia Leigh

At Grubby's Burger Joint, J.J. held the door for Suzy, then said, "Yo," and flicked a wave at a huddle of sophomores playing cards in a bright red booth. He ushered her to the only table available, a little two-seater right in the middle.

Loud voices echoed off the turquoise and white tiled floor, and herds of teens, parents, and kids milled around, ordering burgers and fries, sharing milkshakes, and self-serving at the soda fountain. Dice clattered across a table from another booth followed by cheers and jeers. A solid wood shelf held tattered books, magazines, and board games, along with a sign for donations and respect for property. Grub, the owner, encouraged loitering as long as there were no fights and no alcohol. One whiff, and he'd call the cops.

Suzy picked up her order, a regular cheeseburger, a peanut butter milkshake, and large fries and met J.J. back at the table. She eyed her heaping tray of fried goodness with a watering mouth until J.J. lifted his lonely, clear cup of ice water with a lemon wedge. *Oink.* He probably thought she was a ginormous pig.

"You're not hungry?" Her cheeks tingled with embarrassment as she slouched into the red chair. Why was he here with her? His unruly hair plus smooth, olive skin, plus broad shoulders, plus, plus, plus.

"Nah, Mom grilled steaks and spuds for dinner. I'm stuffed." He traced circles in the water that dripped off his

Play Games by Stacia Leigh 6.30.17

78

THREE

Their
Hell
Reached
Extra
Ears.

One-Word Prompt: Acrostic

Hanging Around for You

EPITAPH

Mother was normal,
and normal left the building.

One-Word Prompt: Epitaph

WITH VISION

Under his feet
the trail grew plentiful
with vision.

One-Word Prompt: Grid

Dealing with Blue

ALL IN

Her painted fingernails
couldn't let go
of the honey.

One-Word Prompt: Grip

CHAPTER 2

DARK AND LIGHT

Miki's hair hung straight and sleek all the way to her waist. Everyone loved it, her friends as well as her frenemies, and it wasn't because she had the longest hair in the junior class. Nope. Try the entire high school. Well, she used to. It used to be a shiny black, the same as her dad's.

Not anymore.

The plump hairdresser, decked out in polka dots and pinup heels, whisked the dark cape away with a flourish, then combed her painted fingernails through Miki's tresses, as if she couldn't let go of her masterpiece, her baby. Miki stared wide-eyed into the mirror and even after three grueling hours in the swivel chair, she still didn't move. Finally, with tentative hands, she sifted through the blunt ends that swung around her shoulders.

"You like it, don't you, honey?" The hairdresser's thinly sculpted brows edged up into her bumper bangs. "It's what you wanted, right?"

It was. Mermaid Blue like the picture. Aqua ends that graduated up to her natural black roots.

all in by Stacia Leigh   12/28/19

9

ATMOSPHERIC PRESSURE

Too much truth was all wrong,
like weird problems I can't talk about.

One-Word Prompt: Simile

Dealing with Blue

Too much too soon? all wrong. like weird. problems I can't talk about.

SPLASH

Nudity and a misunderstanding
splashed in the water.

🏳 *One-Word Prompt: Collage*

UNPLUGGED

Quiet as ever,
nobody could hear his heart talk.

🚩 *One-Word Prompt: Nature*

Stacia Leigh

unplugged by Stacia Leigh   8/25/24

STACIA LEIGH

...grew up in the Flathead Valley and domiciles in the Pacific Northwest with a flock of chickens, two rescue mutts, several artists, and a very special computer nerd.

She's an award-winning, independent author and publisher, currently writing what she loves to read: flirty romances that are light on the angst and heavy on the fun.

Want to learn more about her upcoming books and latest projects or to swing by for a quick hello? Boom! Done. All you have to do is visit her here:

www.stacialeigh.com

* * *

NARWHAL

I'm spreading wonder
with one word.

One-Word Prompt: Twist

Dealing with Blue

"No, I don't." J.J. shuddered.

"Alright, *Charlie*, what's your answer?"

"Oh, right, I'm Charlie. Let's see, I don't sing in the shower because I'm boring, but I do like to yodel while I'm on the toilet, laying cable…how's that for a visual?"

"You're gross." She wrinkled her nose.

"*Charlie's* gross. But if you're asking me, I don't sing in the shower, either. I'm a thinker. I get some of my best ideas while I'm spreading lather all over my body." He rubbed his hands over his chest and moaned.

"You're impossible." Suzy squeezed her eyes shut and laughed. He laughed, too. "Okay, your turn. Pretend I'm Gemma. What would you ask?"

J.J.'s laugh ended abruptly. He scratched his head and ran his fingers through his unruly mane. No wonder it stood on end, not that she minded or anything.

He glanced up with his eyes set to stun. They radiated a beautiful green, light and dark and mesmerizing. She'd better buck up her personal fortress because that one look had her dazzled.

"What I want to ask *you*," he said, "is do you wanna take a drive on Friday?" Suzy couldn't tear her eyes away from him. What if…? No. He was Mr. Cool, all laid back, easy and fun, and he was being good for his word. What if…? No. She was stuck and dirty and contaminated. An hour ago she'd pulled a dead animal out of her house.

What if…?

No.

Narwhal by Maria Leigh 12/3/17

177

Behind the blackout poems and doodle art are three young adult love stories with flirt, grit, and small town fun. Don't miss out!

Dealing with Blue
by
Stacia Leigh

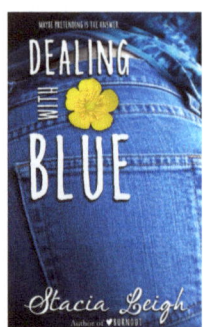

"Name your price, Suzy Blue. Everyone's got one."— Life used to be normal until Suzy Blue moves into the trailer park with her mom. Then things turn secretive and claustrophobic. To get out of the house, Suzy accepts a deal with the charming neighbor boy, J.J. Radborne. All he needs is a pretend girlfriend for bonfires, fun, and a possible prom date, and all she needs is driving lessons to get out of this town...for good.

"You're making a huge mistake, J.J."— So says Gemma, J.J.'s ex-girlfriend. She's turning up the heat in a confusing mind game, and J.J. knows exactly who to team up with: Suzy Blue. She's cute, convenient, and even sorta funny. More importantly, Gemma's already jealous. Hey, she started it; he's just playing along. So, yeah. Suzy…perfect. Now, if she'd only cooperate.

Dealing with Blue is a small town love story set in the Pacific Northwest. It's about a strong girl and a bad boy peeling back the layers to discover what's true.

FINALIST 2015 PNWA Literary Contest for Young Adults
FINALIST 2016 PNWA Nancy Pearl Book Award

ISBN: 978-0-6926088-1-4

Burnout
by
Stacia Leigh

"I have a plan."— Miki Holtz isn't some rebellious sixteen-year-old just because she dyed her hair blue and rides a motorcycle. She's an independent girl who knows what, when, and how to get things done… almost. She can't seem to gain her dad's attention or make a connection with her soul crush, Will Sullivan. But when her dad invites her along to the Burnout Biker Rally—and Will is going, too—she jumps at the chance to turn her luck around.

"I don't like the way you like me."— While grieving the death of his mom, Will Sullivan has turned into an undeniable couch potato until he's forced on a road trip with his dad's motorcycle buddies as some kind of biker therapy. What's worse? He's paired up with the prez's daughter, Miki, a girl who once humiliated him in front of his friends—a girl he can't forgive…or forget.

Burnout is an adventure story set in the Pacific Northwest where a strong girl and a moody boy discover love while trying to survive on a road trip from hell.

FINALIST for Young Adult in the 2016 PNWA Literary Contest under the title *Riding with the Hides of Hell*.

ISBN: 978-1-7321435-0-0

Hanging Around for You
by Stacia Leigh

"Forget something?" — Abandoned by her free-spirited mother, Pinecone Rudd has been left with the only "family" she's got, her mom's ex-boyfriend, a seasoned biker named Hammond Barba. Together, they're hiding a grievous secret, which has Pinecone making up stories like everything is wonderful. But when a new, good-looking senior named Beau Smiley shows up at school asking questions and hanging around, things begin to unravel. He is definitely one to keep an eye on. Except every time she looks his way, he's got his eye on her, too.

"Play it smart." — Beau Smiley is in the middle of a dangerous game, working for one motorcycle club while spying on another. Acting like a rat is not a life goal but a temporary gig for some fast money. The plus side: getting close to the bohemian beauty, Pinecone Rudd. She's a person of interest…in more ways than one. The down side: potentially falling for this girl while deceiving her at every turn. That's why he created rules for himself, like rule #2: no distractions. Too bad he's not very good at following them.

Hanging Around for You is a small town love story set in the Pacific Northwest where lies and spies bring an independent girl and a risk-taking boy closer together.

ISBN: 978-1-7321435-2-4

Blackout Poetry & Art BINGO

ZIG ZAG	LAYER	SEASON	BUBBLE	DREAM
WILD	RHYME	WATER	FLIRT	HAIKU
DIRT	CROSS	FREE	EAT	LADDER
SECRET	GLUE	TIC-TAC-TOE	SORROW	PLAY
ANAGRAM	TAROT	WALL	METAPHOR	STIPPLING

Use these one-word prompts to spark your artistic energy. It's Bingo time! For a quick win, make 5 blackout poems in a row—up, down, or diagonal—or go for a solid blackout and make 25. Most importantly, explore and enjoy the process of creating.

www.StaciaLeigh.com

www.ingramcontent.com/pod-product-compliance
Lightning Source LLC
Chambersburg PA
CBHW041307110426
42743CB00037B/23